THE WEB 3.0 MARKETING REVOLUTION

SHAUN MATHIESON

ISBN: 978-0-646-87282-7

"A brand is no longer what we tell the consumer it is; it's what consumers tell each other it is."

Scott Cook

Co-founder Intuit

CONTENTS

FOREWORD

THE INTERNET AS WE KNOW IT IS CHANGING

Whether we like it or not, the World Wide Web has been instrumental in our evolution as modern humans. From what started as a system of information retrieval has today evolved into one of the world's most powerful tools that is used by billions of people around the world every day.

In December 1995 there were an estimated 16 million active Internet users.[1] Compare that to today where more than half of the world's population in 2022, estimated to be over 5 billion people, use the Internet as part of their every day life.[2]

The primary reason for the explosion in users

today is our reliance on the Internet for news, information and entertainment, coupled with the rise in mobile technology which makes the Internet all the more accessible.

Most of us barely even realise that our lives have already moved almost completely online. Research has been published that the average mobile phone user can interact with their device up to 2,617 times per day and those average number of interactions more than doubles for the top 10% of users at over 5,400 per day, equivalent to almost 4 hours of screen time.[3]

With over 60 percent of the world's total population constantly accessing the Internet by using streaming services, social media, or simply asking Google where to find the best burger in town, our reliance on the Internet permeates throughout almost every aspect of our daily lives.

In 2023, you can't have marketing without the Internet. Marketers for the better part of the last two decades have relied increasingly upon the Internet for advertising and consumer research. Without the

Internet, marketers and the brands that they represent, would have little to no way of knowing just what the effectiveness of their campaigns look like and, specifically, how the consumer responds to it.

Thanks to the Internet, marketers can decipher the previously indecipherable. Things like consumer habits and behaviours can be more easily scrutinised and understood from the data that we each share online. So where do we go to from here, when everything marketers have grown accustomed to is about to change?

Web 3.0 is the next generation of the Internet, and it promises to revolutionise the very way that marketers use the web to promote their brands and businesses.

There are a number of changes currently taking place that every brand, business and marketer need to be aware of in order to succeed in the future. Marketers must adapt their strategies now for Web 3.0 and learn to embrace completely new technologies and ideas before they get left behind by their competitors. This includes everything from AI-powered tools, to virtual reality and augmented/mixed reality, cryptocurrency, blockchains and more.

Staying on the cutting edge of technology and remaining up-to-date with the change that it brings means that brands will have to identify new ways to provide their customers with the best possible experience, or otherwise risk being quickly seen as old or out-dated.

In much the same way that the rise of Web 2.0 and social media had a profound impact on the way we communicate and interact with one another, the trend towards Web 3.0 and user-generated content will continue as we move into the next phase of the Internet's evolution.

Web 3.0, sometimes referred to as the Semantic Web, looks to be even more collaborative and user-friendly than its predecessor. With the help of artificial intelligence, businesses will be better able to understand customer needs while delivering relevant information and unique, personalised experiences for each customer.

The changes that we are currently seeing are just the beginning and the true potential of Web 3.0 has yet to be fully realised. Over the last decade there has been a steady shift away from traditional advertising methods, and a greater uptake in content marketing.

Content in 2023 is the cornerstone of any marketing effort, and brands must now actively produce enough of it to be able to keep up with demand and the expectations of consumers. Brands therefore are being built and maintained on social media, and for a business to flourish online, their creative content must also flourish.

Social media is still one of the most underpriced ways that marketers can attract new audiences and get their brands recognised around the world. Prior to the Internet, people were connected through relationships. The old adage 'six degrees of separation' meant that networking in social circles was key to meeting new people and making new contacts.

However, with the Internet, in particular Web

2.0, we witnessed a global change as we could more easily connect with people from around the world through common interests, beliefs and causes; such as a particular subject, event, celebrity, and the list goes on.

This equation centred around people's interests has given rise to social media platforms like Tik Tok, that rewards the user for their interests by showing them more content based on that interest.

New technologies and social media platforms are constantly emerging and are creating a whole new landscape for businesses to adapt to. As a result, traditional marketing methods are no longer as effective as they used to be.

Moreover, traditional experiences that businesses provide their customers are also rapidly evolving, as brands are now having to provide meaningful personalisations for their customers across a growing number of touchpoints. This requires a significant investment by the business into its brand, while at the same time keeping a long-term focus about what sets their brand apart from competitors. This means thinking about the lifetime value of a customer, rather than just focusing on short-term sales and interim profit.

With millions of people around the world playing a part in this new online customer ecosystem, marketers need to re-think how they provide on-going value. New ideas centred around Non-fungible Tokens (NFTs) can offer insights into how marketers and brands can adapt for the future now, and in this book we're going to touch on exactly what some of these new ideas look like and what brands should be doing today to take advantage of the change that's to come.

As you become familiar with new worlds like cryptocurrency and blockchains it may seem overwhelming at first. But remember, it is not necessary to know every aspect of crypto or blockchains to understand what Web 3.0 is and what it will likely entail. Do you know how the current Internet (Web 2.0) works? Probably not. And yet, you navigate it daily with ease; searching, shopping, connecting with friends, and so much more.

CHAPTER 1

MARKETING *VS* ADVERTISING

Marketing is a relatively broad term which basically describes everything marketers do that advertises a brand, product or service. However, there is a distinct and often misunderstood difference between what is 'marketing' and what is 'advertising'.

Many marketers will argue that advertising falls under the marketing umbrella, but in truth, they work alongside each other for the benefit of the overall brand and business. Marketing in its very essence is the careful consideration that goes in to ensuring that products or services are placed in front of the right people at the right time. As one of the primary functions of businesses, its importance has grown exponentially in recent years as companies increasingly look to reach new audiences and better understand their customers. Marketing, therefore, is simply a balance of theory and practice, while advertising is the tangible steps taken to achieve a pre-determined goal.

Advertising is *doing*, marketing is knowing *why* to do it

Early forms of advertising can be traced back to ancient civilizations, where merchants would promote their wares through oral storytelling and simple signs.

By the Middle Ages, advertising had become a bit more sophisticated, with the use of town criers and hand-written pamphlets. The invention of the printing press in the 15th century ushered in a new era of advertising, as mass-produced newspapers, flyers and pamphlets allowed the widespread dissemination of information and ideas. The 18th century saw

Image Credit: M Abnodey, pexels.com

The Romans used to advertise Gladiator events which would regularly feature fighting figures and sometimes gory scenes to increase excitement and encourage attendance of spectators. The world's first-ever written advertisement is thought to be a papryus discovered among the ruins of Thebes in Egypt. Dating back to 3000 BC, it was created by a slaveholder attempting to locate a runaway slave while also promoting their weaving business.

The Five W's

MARKETING	ADVERTISING
Who	**What**
Why	**When**
	Where

Who *are we targeting?*

Why *is this going to benefit them?*

What *methods will we use to reach them?*

When *is the best time to reach them?*

Where *will they see this campaign?*

further innovations, such as the advent of primitive advertising agencies not long before the 19th century industrial revolution resulted in a boom of advertising services that could reach far and wide audiences. The 20th century saw even more advances, with the rise of radio, television, and notably, Internet advertising.

Today, advertising is more prevalent than ever before, reaching into every corner of our lives and has become a pervasive by-product of consumerism where brands are forced to stand out against hundreds, if not thousands, of competitors. Marketing, on the other hand, is inherently research-based, and is about collecting and aggregating different types of data that helps to understand who the customer is and why they need what we're offering.

Prior to the invention of the Internet, collecting customer data was primarily done through physical research tactics like product trials, questionnaires and the like. The in-depth research and customer data that the Internet has allowed marketers has completely transformed the advertising landscape. Businesses that better understand their customers can more easily determine how, where, and when to spend their advertising money.

Common marketing objectives today are to increase brand awareness or sales, enter new markets, or to launch new products, however in order to achieve these objectives, marketing campaigns need to be carefully designed and implemented. A marketing campaign is essentially a series of planned activities with a specific purpose, such as raising awareness or generating sales. Campaigns will usually consist of several key elements: research (to understand the target market), planning (to develop strategies and tactics), implementation (to carry out the plan), and evaluation (to assess results).

Marketing campaigns can be small and local, or large and global. They can also be short-term or long-term, or they might only run at very specific times of the year because that's when they are most likely to appeal to consumers. The most important thing is that they are closely aligned with the business' goals so that marketers can effectively measure their campaigns and demonstrate return on investment (ROI).

The Internet has helped us to better understand consumers

Both marketing and advertising are the building blocks of every successful brand, and in 2023 the Internet is the mortar that holds it all together. As more and more people use the Internet and other digital devices on a daily basis, companies have had to change their marketing strategies to adapt to the ever-evolving online landscape.

Traditional advertising channels such as TV commercials and print ads are no longer as effective as they once were because people are now spending more time online than ever before. This shift has led to the rise of technology and programs that enable marketers to deliver powerful advertising to better reach and understand their consumers. Thanks to the

The 4 Key Pillars of Successful Marketing Campaigns:

RESEARCH
Understanding the target market

↓

PLANNING
Development of strategies and advertising tactics

↓

IMPLEMENTATION
Carrying out the plan

↓

EVALUATION
Assessing the results

Internet, marketers today have access to a multitude of data that can help businesses of all sizes define audiences, target consumers, find opportunities, and generate revenue. But it wasn't always easy.

In the Web 1.0 world of the late 90's and early 2000's, if you could demonstrate that your site had excellent traffic and regular visitors, that would pretty much be enough to convince someone that advertising on your site was a smart idea. There was almost no way then of knowing the specific demographics of the audience or consumer that browsed each website. If your website was about fast cars and how great they are, you'd probably assume that the audience would be largely made up of car fanatics and rev-heads.

Gaining an understanding of the type of user your website attracts is quick and simple today thanks to services such as Google Analytics. Google has grown so far beyond its beginnings as a search engine to being more-or-less the facilitator of the Internet for many who browse online today. As the favourite and primary search engine of the world, Google is a powerhouse of data and analytics and its impact on marketing has been profound. It is almost unimaginable to think of an Internet without Google so it is no surprise that they hold enormous amounts of our data and why so many corporations and businesses actively seek it to better understand consumers online habits and how they interact with websites. Google Analytics is incredibly easy to set up and within a few minutes you can be tracking your website's traffic which has proved so popular that it is used by just over 55% of all websites online today.[1]

Data, data, everywhere...

The extensive collection of online data has served as the basis of almost all advertising in the current Web 2.0 environment and there are many benefits from a marketing perspective. First, it can help to segment audiences more effectively into certain groups or categories. By targeting small groups of people with specific interests, rather than trying to reach everyone all at once, allows marketers to get more creative with advertising and tailor content to specific demographics and interests.

Data can also help track results and improve marketing campaigns over time, tracking which messages are working and then adjusting the strategy or creative accordingly. As a consumer, we are constantly generating and sharing data online. This data also enables us a more seamless experience when browsing the Internet.

These days we may begrudgingly accept 'cookies' on websites we visit because we know the data we share with a website can actually serve a purpose. Whether it's ads with discount codes for things we would, or do actually buy, or even something as seemingly simple as keeping track of all the items we've placed in our online shopping cart. You will get the best user experience from a website if you accept cookies, whereas declining cookies may affect your experience. Cookies are essentially small blocks of data that track a variety of information online about users habits such as what websites they have visited recently, websites they visit frequently, what they've searched for on Google, and even on-site behaviour such as where they click, scroll speed and even where their mouse hovered.

Marketers use this data to formulate opinions on the type of audiences attracted to their website, what they're looking for and how best to convert them into a paying customer. But data like this doesn't just arrive, first you have to lure potential customers in, and then secondly, they have to trust your brand enough to want to share that data with you.

Engage the consumer and build trust

Advertising can only go so far as to arouse attention, or emotion, from a viewer that results in a desired action including; filling out a contact form, becoming an online subscriber, or purchasing a product etc.

At the same time, trust has to be built between the brand and the potential customer in order to increase the likelihood of the desired result. Historically, we have done this through the sharing of knowledge and information and uploading it as online content to offer value directly to the consumer without prior engagement.

Blogs, how-to videos, product reviews and more, are just some of the many popular ways in which marketers use content to be able to increase views and engagement with a brand or business, while at the same time building trust with audiences new and old. Today, content is the cornerstone of marketing strategies for businesses big and small all over the world, and it is all thanks to the Internet.

The Internet has allowed marketers to gain insights into the customer and their journey in ways we could never have imagined with Web 1.0, which has resulted in enormous amounts of mainstream and niche content being produced.

Following the Web 2.0 evolution and the rapid

rise of social media, we saw an even greater connection with consumers through creating highly-shareable online content with the ability to go 'viral' and reach millions of new potential customers.

Understanding customers' pain-points has been critical to the creation of helpful and engaging content from both a marketing and advertising perspective. Different types of online content will always attract different types of customers, but the more content you can create, the more potential customers you can attract to your website or social media page.

Smart marketers will generate data by running frequent tests using different types of content to see which produces a better result, or what resonates more with their target audience. In the end, enormous amounts of data will be accumulated from which future advertising campaigns will be built.

This constant collection of data has sparked numerous debates about online privacy, and many industry experts are anticipating this will be a key aspect of the approaching Web evolution.

To foresee what changes we can expect in the not-too-distant future with Web 3.0, let's take a look back at how the Internet began, how it evolved, and what brands did at the time to stay ahead of the curve.

CHAPTER 2

A BRIEF HISTORY OF THE INTERNET

The Internet has only been around for a relatively short period of time, but it has quickly become one of the most used tools by businesses, marketers and individuals globally.

Although the origins of the Internet date back to at least the 1970's, it was not until 1990 that the term 'World Wide Web' would be coined. In 1989 Tim Berners-Lee, one of the fathers of the Internet we know today, proposed the idea of linked information systems connected by 'hypertext'. Hypertext is described by Berners-Lee as "human-readable information linked together in an unconstrained way." In short, this would allow all staff within his organisation, including managers and stakeholders, to search for information, documents and more through a computer system using only keywords.

This invention changed the Internet from a simple network of computers to what could be a global platform for information exchange. For the first time in our history we were able to use technology to instantly summon information at lightning speed using only our fingertips.

The Internet as we know it was born

We take for granted the ability we have to search the Internet for answers to our burning questions, whether it's searching directions to a friend's house, or for reviews about a product before we make a purchase, the Internet has given us a one-stop-shop for almost all of our daily needs.

What is second nature to us today was revolutionary at the time of its creation. The original 'World

Wide Web', which we'll refer to as Web 1.0, would not be visually recognisable to most Internet users today. When browsing in the very early days of Web 1.0 you'd be greeted with an overwhelming amount of plain text, only minimal graphics, and almost no UX/UI enhancements which we expect today. After you spent a good few minutes 'dialling on' to the Internet, users would often only see a set of clearly written instructions and links to click on, or keywords to search that could take you to your desired destination.

It wasn't until 1993 that the first graphical web browser Mosaic would be launched. Hailed as the first widely downloaded Internet browser and hugely popular among 'non-techies', the Mosaic browser offered users a seamless and much more aesthetic way of browsing and interacting with the Internet.

Not long after in 1996, two Stanford University students Larry Page and Sergy Bin, as part of their Ph. D research project, would create a software system that could crawl the Internet more efficiently and produce better results than existing search engines like

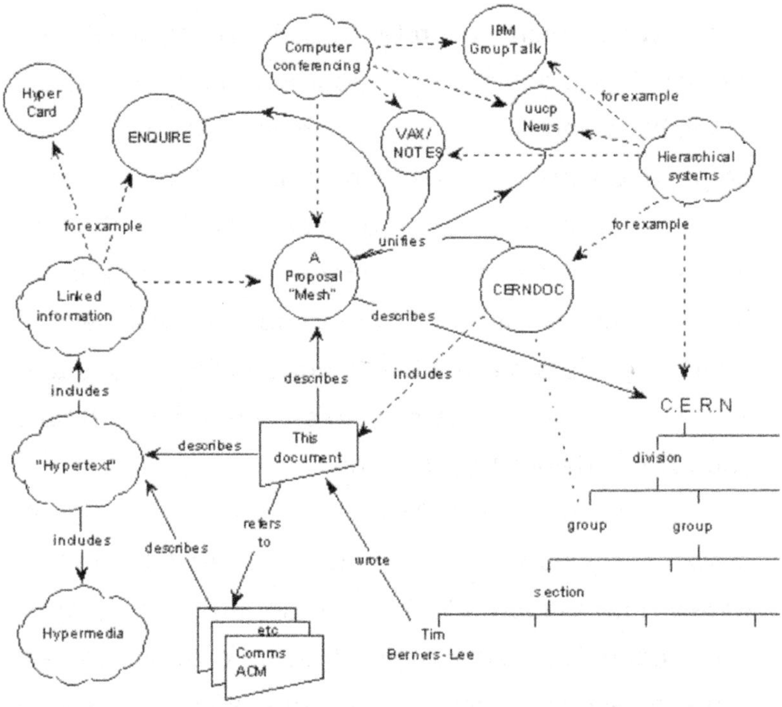

Tim Berners-Lee's internet was a system of interlinked hypertext documents that allowed users to quickly locate and access information while working at CERN, the European Organization for Nuclear Research. It was made possible by HTML, the hypertext markup language, which Berners-Lee developed to store and structure web content

Mosaic. One year later Larry and Sergy would launch Google.

The early days of the Internet is often referred to as the 'read-only' web. It was mostly static pages with no ability yet to log-in to a webpage, view analytics or interact with posts. For this reason, we can think of Web 1.0 as one big Encyclopedia where users could search for something and browse the results.

Dawn of the age of information

Between 1990 and 1997, the number of households in the United States that owned personal computers were steadily increasing. During this time computer ownership increased from 15% to 35%[1] marking the shift to the Information Age, an online economy based on information-sharing platforms and the dawn of countless new sub-industries.

With personal and home computer ownership being seen less as a luxury item and more of a household necessity, we were quickly becoming a society more adept at navigating the Internet and the new ways in which we could benefit from it.

In 1997, Hotmail became one of the first webmail services on the Internet, offering users a free web-based e-mail address and the ability to seamlessly and instantaneously write to our friends, family and associates from around the globe. We could also access this e-mail account from anywhere in the world. Hotmail would go on to become the world's largest webmail service with more than 30 million active users by 1999 and eventually be bought out by Microsoft for $400million.[2]

Thousands more people were logging on every week to access the wealth of information that Web 1.0 provided and it was clear that both the Internet and the desires of its users were changing. While many were still resisting the Internet gold-rush, forward-thinking companies were looking for ways to take advantage of growing audiences and private investment interest. Advertisers and marketers could also see clearly the enormous revenue potential of a growing online consumer base and the power it had to communicate individual brands.

At that time, Web 1.0 was a very one-directional experience for users, businesses and early digital advertisers. With no defined audiences or ways in which to reach a specific type of customer, advertisers needed a way to stand out to a highly passive audience.

Say hello to the first-ever online banner ad

In the early 90's, a small rectangle advertisement, closely resembling what we would today call a 'leaderboard' banner, was purchased by AT&T on HotWired.com. This ad was to form part of AT&T's "You Will" campaign, which included a series of television commercials showing scenes from an Internet-enabled future.

The static banner they created was simple yet effective. Featuring distinctly coloured text on a

AT&T's first digital advertising campaign went live in 1997, with the launch of its "You Will" campaign. The campaign, which ran for nearly two years, was designed to emphasise the connection between AT&T, its customers and the power of future technology.

black background that asked the viewer if they've ever clicked their mouse HERE and then an arrow pointing to YOU WILL. Even more remarkable was the fact that the ad was clicked by about 44% of all people who saw it.[3]

Advertising digitally would catch on quickly and in 1995 Yahoo.com would trial their own primitive advertising technique that showcased the logos of their five main sponsor companies, rotating daily atop of Yahoo's website.

Because of the one-way nature of Web 1.0, personal websites were finding increasing popularity among more experienced Internet users and acted as an outlet for those looking to build a community of like-minded people. These personal websites were the very beginnings of what we know today as blogs and would later give rise to Web 2.0 and the prevalence of social media.

Your own personal place on the Web

Some of the oldest websites still operating today started life as a personal site or an online community in the early days of the Internet. The history of personal websites on the Internet can be traced back to the early days of Geocities.com and Angelfire.com.

These early websites were typically basic webpages that served as a digital business card or resume. In the late 1990s and early 2000s, personal websites became more popular with the advent of easy-to-use web authoring tools and hosting services. The use of personal websites waned in the mid-2000s as social networking sites such as MySpace and Facebook rose to prominence. However, in recent years there has been a resurgence in interest in personal websites, spurred on by the popularity of microblogging platforms such as Twitter and Tumblr.

Whereas Web 1.0 was largely dominated by brands and companies showcasing themselves or their products, Web 2.0 would usher in a new era of interactivity where everyday people from all over the world could edit, publish and share content online in more ways than ever before.

CHAPTER 3

WEB 2.0 AND THE SHARING ECONOMY

By the late 1990's, the Dot Com Boom was in full swing. There was real hysteria amongst investors trying to capitalise on soaring stock prices of publicly listed technology companies before the bubble finally burst in 2000, which left many start-ups, among other tech companies at the time out of business. The few that survived we still know to this day and in fact make up some of the largest and most powerful companies in the world like Apple, Microsoft and Amazon.

The majority of survivors of the crash that took place either built the technology/software or materials related to Internet and computer usage, or had a sound business plan to thrive in the emerging online retail sector. News publications would also find success online. Being able to reach an ever-growing audience appealed to traditional print media outlets, as well as realising the lucrative ability to generate new streams of advertising revenue.

Reach as many people as possible

Advertising became the default business model on the Internet because it was the easiest way for companies and start-ups to earn revenue and show profit.

Start-ups which could attribute revenue growth to a network of online ads were proving that they were worthy of private investment to take their business to the next level. However, what many were actually focusing on was something else entirely.

Instead of selling a specific product or service online, future-savvy brands at the time sought to first establish as big of an audience as they possibly could. Their theory was simple – a website with tens of millions of loyal visitors would surely find a way to generate revenue.

Already successful companies that were at least a decade away from taking full advantage of the Internet also still needed a presence online in order to build their brand and future-proof their business. They started the same way as many did; provide enough value to an audience that they return to your website and, hopefully, eventually become customers.

In 2001 the tide was well and truly turning with the launch of Wikipedia which began paving the way for collective web content and knowledge sharing, leading to the foundations of the sharing economy we know today. This burgeoning economy based on peer-to-peer sharing was becoming more commonplace on the Internet with the likes of Napster, one of the original file sharing websites, which achieved notoriety after being shut down by a court order for copyright claims made by powerful music industry moguls. Along with accusations that Napster was impacting music industry sales, there were those that believed file sharing on Napster actually stimulated, rather than hurt, sales.

It was also now possible for us to share our opinions, dreams, feelings, and thoughts, as well as the things that we were doing on a daily basis. MySpace, a social media platform which launched in 2003, offered users the chance to display their unique personality and their place in the world. This period in time marked the evolution from Web 1.0 to Web 2.0, also known as the 'Social Web'.

The evolution that was taking place provided a two-way experience of the Internet. Instead of the one-directional nature of Web 1.0, the Social Web or Web 2.0, allowed users to read, write, and publish content on the Internet. They could also communicate like never before, establishing whole communities that were entirely online – hence the name the 'Social Web' due to the millions of people around the world who played a part in creating it. During this time, not only could we seek information from web pages, but the web pages themselves could seek information from us.

With the newly-dawning age of social media, huge amounts of data were being collected and harnessed by central corporations to produce even better results for companies who wanted to advertise online. This is still happening today, although on a much greater scale, largely owed to the development of online marketing techniques.

Digital marketing takes the stage

Traditionally, ads on Web 1.0 were targeted according to the content with which they appeared, not to the demographic or profile of the user, as is common today. However, in the early 2000's it was becoming possible to analyse users' personal websites in order to better target ads. Although this would initially prove risky – or risqué?

Before marketers could use data to target audiences, Ethan Zuckerman created the first vertically-oriented advertisement in the form of a pop-up window. This was intended to be a less intrusive way of advertising than inserting an ad into the centre of a user's homepage. Zuckerman's pop-up window was actually a solution to a problem when a major car company at the time found out that they'd bought a banner ad on a page that celebrated anal sex.

Associating an ad with a user's page, without putting it directly on the page, meant that advertisers and marketers wouldn't need to worry about a viewer making an affiliation between their brand and the page's content.

Harnessing habits with data

With all this data pouring in from personal websites and social media profiles, marketers could engage with and understand their audiences like never before, and now with a new online advertising tool-kit they were reaching more people than ever before.

As we browsed Web 2.0 by viewing Facebook

pages, watching videos online and performing Google searches, we were unknowingly sharing our data with large corporations who would use the data to better serve us ads and content based on our browsing habits. While this of course leads to a better user-experience, it has also sparked many debates about data privacy.

Web 2.0 is the web we are most familiar with and it is also the web that has, for better or worse, given us targeted advertising. One famous example of the power of targeted advertising that we hear time and again is that of someone who's been served pregnancy-related ads before they even knew they were pregnant.

In his 2012 article for the New York Times, Charles Duhigg discusses how Target hooks expecting couples just before they become parents.[1] By creating a history of everything a customer purchased from them or from other sources, Target would assign shoppers a Guest ID number, linked to their credit card, name, or e-mail address. Then, they could cross-examine historical buying data of Target baby registry customers to see if any patterns emerged.

Due to the fact that birth records are usually public, new parents are almost instantly bombarded with offers and incentives. The key to Target's marketing strategy was to reach them sooner, before any other retailers or competitors find out that a baby is on its way. Ads that were designed to appeal to women during their second trimester for example, when many pregnant women begin buying all sorts of products in preparation for their arrival, could therefore expect to have a greater chance of conversion.

In the end, Target's computers were able to identify approximately 25 products that, when analysed together, allowed them to assign a pregnancy prediction score to each shopper. Eerily, they were also able to estimate their due date within a short timeframe, which allowed Target to send strategic coupons, discounts and advertisements at specific stages of pregnancy.

Duhigg suggests that Target's revenue growth of $44 billion in 2002, to $67 billion in 2010,[2] is largely attributed to the retail giant harnessing data in this way.

But it's not only our online shopping habits or Google searches that contribute to this form of data collection. Everything we consume online gives a particular impression of the stage we are at in life, or the types of topics and content we are interested in.

With an endless source of content being uploaded, Web 2.0 has provided the perfect platform for corporations like Facebook to capture large amounts of data which can be used to the advantage of brands and marketers. Consequently, a users 'newsfeed' on Facebook may appear totally different from another person due to the information that has been collected about each of them.

Web 2.0 has taught us how to gather, share and interpret this information to be able to use it to segment audiences which has enabled marketers to make strategic decisions when it comes to advertising brands.

Social media has already had a profound impact on the way we communicate and interact with one another, and as we move faster toward the Web 3.0 world, we can expect even more changes in the way we consume and create what has become one of the Internet's most important resources – content.

CHAPTER 4

CREATING CONTENT TO INFLUENCE AUDIENCES

Every day we are consuming content. It comes in all shapes and sizes, whether it's a funny cat video, or someone's top ten tips on growing grapes, the amount of content uploaded to the Internet is increasing with each and every minute. In fact, so much content was being uploaded in the early days of Web 2.0 that certain measures had to be taken in order to manage the massive amounts of content being uploaded and stored on the Internet.

When we moved from Web 1.0 to Web 2.0, blogging had just become a mainstream outlet and a new-found affinity for anyone with something to say.

Experts believe a gentleman by the name of Justin Hall started the world's first blog in 1994 where he wrote about art that he enjoyed while also showcasing work of his own.[1] This form of self-expression was often referred to as "online diaries" and LiveJournal was one of the most popular places on the Internet for people to voice an opinion or share a personal life story.

My blogger, my keeper

In 2005, Garrett Graff became the first blogger in the world to be granted a White House press pass.[2] This was a big deal at the time as it signalled audiences gravitating away from traditional news outlets and major media corporations to hear news and opinions from independent voices.

Today, blogs are still a crucial element to marketing strategies for all types of businesses and are easily one of the best ways to leverage search engine optimization (SEO). By regularly posting blogs and sharing thoughts on industry trends and news, as well as behind-the-scenes insights into their own teams and culture, companies are able to direct traffic to their websites and start engaging with their customers in more ways than one.

Blogs are essentially tools to 'sell without selling'. Brands can cleverly position themselves as credible sources of information on topics related to their industry, if they only create the content that is of value to their target audience.

However, not everyone has the resources or the time to write hundreds of blogs, or devise countless scripts for videos. As such, brands have to strike a balance between showcasing their own content as well as incorporating select pieces created by others. This is often referred to as 'content curation' and involves sharing content from relevant third parties. This is not to claim other people's content as the brand's own, but when done right and properly citing the original owner, it can greatly help expand the audience and reach of a brand.

Having content on your website is an important step in ensuring your online presence is effective and results in sales. Consumers need to be engaged at every step of their customer journey, and a brand needs to be constantly front-of-mind in order to be considered at decision time. Content therefore can greatly aid in how people discover new brands and businesses while also assisting in the overall decision-making process. Product reviews, customer testimonials and the like, can help establish enormous trust at a crucial moment in the research and decision stage of the consumer's journey.

Content becomes king

To remain relevant, brands in the early days of Web 2.0 had to maintain a consistent stream of content that is interesting, valuable, and easy to share with others.

As Internet access continued to grow around the world throughout the mid 2000's, marketers were constantly finding new and creative ways to reach larger audiences and increase advertising return on investment (ROI).

During the current age of information overload, fictional stories in advertising have become somewhat redundant and unrealistic, and are no longer solely required to imagine an experience with a product. Traditionally, advertising has for a long time focused on the experience of the product through fictional storytelling. Coca-Cola, for instance, spent years telling Santa Claus and polar bear stories to great effect, and are even credited with reinventing the visual portrayal of Santa Claus into the jolly, rosy-cheeked character we know today. Instead, consumers want to hear directly from real people who have actually used the product or service. In fact, consumers today will even actively seek advice from total strangers on Internet forums like Reddit before considering a service or making a decision to purchase a product.

The Internet, and indeed social media networks, have made it easier for everyday people to share their experiences and as a result, fictional advertising has been replaced by non-fictional advertising in the form of user-generated content (UGC).

It's no secret that UGC has been on the rise since social media networks became popular. Unlike purposeful advertising, which is designed and delivered in accordance with a specific marketing campaign, UGC comes from the people in the form of engagement with a brand based on its merits or disadvantages using Facebook posts, Twitter posts, YouTube videos, and so much more.

It could be said that most of what we see on social media is actually UGC, and in one way or another promotes a brand or service whether directly or in-directly.

For example, you might be browsing your Facebook newsfeed and notice a friend who has just posted photos of their recent family trip to the Zoo. What they have posted is heart-warming and personal, but it is also in-directly promoting the Zoo, which may lead to greater consumer awareness and the potential of increased ticket sales.

Another example could be a popular YouTube streamer with thousands of followers. Not only does the streamer provide content that is unique, educational and entertaining, but they're also using the latest equipment from a small selection of brands.

As any marketer will tell you, consistency is key when creating and uploading content. But it takes time and resources to put together so much content for individual platforms and in a range of consumable formats.

Generally, marketers need to aim to be posting up to six pieces of content per day to remain relevant and front-of-mind with consumers. However, this requires an entire team from content creators and graphic designers, to writers, social media managers as well as a head of marketing to oversee the strategy and ensure that there is a constant stream of high-value and eye-catching content. UGC allows brands to be everywhere across each network, and can help fill in the gaps in a marketers content schedule when there is not enough time or resources to continually create new content. It's a dream come true if your brand or business is loved by many, but unfortunately not so good if your public perception is lacking.

Brands today are ever more weary about having to constantly mould their public image and the way they promote UGC, while also ensuring that people's experiences remain positive so as to avoid a bad customer review or experience becoming a negative trending topic online.

Social media has played a key role in introducing brands directly to their audiences and core customer base through the content that users generate. It has also helped shape the way that content is delivered. In the early days of Web 2.0, videos were largely under-utilised until YouTube became more well-known.

Even still, if you were browsing Facebook around 2006, the majority of content and ads you'd see would be in the form of still images, text or basic graphics. In 2023, however, video ads and short-form video content are consistently the top performing format across all of the major social media platforms.

Short videos have been surging in popularity in recent years on platforms such as YouTube, TikTok and Instagram. This could be, in part, courtesy of our time-poor society where we no longer have the time or patience to read a long online article or watch a 10-min video in order to understand a topic. Instead, we've turned our attention to online personalities that we trust and who can deliver short, bite-sized videos as our preferred method of initial research.

The age of influencer marketing

The recent phenomena of social media 'influencers' has essentially taken the same strategy as many start-ups did during the early days of the Dot Com boom. By establishing as big of an audience and online following as possible, these social media influencers can then turn their content into a way of generating income.

As their title suggests, influencers partner

with brands to influence their audiences' purchasing decisions via their social media. Influencers today are regarded as celebrities in their own right. They have followings into the millions, are some of the most recognisable people on the planet, and make generous sums of money whenever they post about a sponsored brand or product. And we listen to them.

It was estimated that approximately 93% of marketers in 2022 used influencers in their campaigns,[3] which is now considered as a key and lucrative advertising strategy.

In fact, a whopping $16.4 billion is forecast to be generated in the influencer marketing industry in 2022, up from $1.7 billion in 2016.[4] There are currently countless brands and businesses that use influencer marketing to get their message out and to help them connect with emerging and established audiences. This is especially helpful if your brand or business is in a niche industry and has a very specific preferred audience.

By partnering with the right influencer, a brand

can make a more genuine impact on consumers' buying behaviour and leave an impression that lasts long after the influencer partnership has ended.

Content and influencer marketing does not produce quick results. It should be viewed as a long-term strategy rather than trying to sell directly to the audience at all times. As such, brands should make their content marketing strategy a key pillar of their business, large and small, to create better lifelong relationships with their customers and remain relevant for years to come. To this end, influencers can help carry a marketing campaign so much further, and often for less spend, than traditional advertising strategies.

In the Algorithm we trust

Propelling all this content forward and into the hands, and eyes, of consumers is the seemingly all-knowing and all-powerful algorithm that social media networks rely on to serve us content it thinks we will like.

The algorithm that Facebook and Instagram use is a complex process that assesses a variety of factors to better deliver targeted content and ads to users. A user's interests, demographics, and even their past interactions with ads will help to determine what a user is most likely to engage with. Based on these interactions, the algorithm will show users content and ads that are more likely to be relevant and engaging to them. This helps businesses reach their target audiences with ads that are more likely to result in conversions.

The first step is identifying the user's interests. This can be done through information that the user has explicitly provided, such as their profile information, or through data that the social media network has collected about their activity on the site. Once interests have been identified, the algorithm will start to show ads and content that are relevant to those interests.

Relevancy is determined by a number of factors, including the ad's target audience, the user's past interactions with similar ads, and the overall quality of the creative or content. Finally, Facebook and Instagram will track how users interact with the ad or content. If they click on it, share it, or take any other action that indicates engagement, then it is deemed successful and will be shown to more users. On the other hand, if users ignore the ad or give it a negative reaction, then it will be less likely to be shown in the future.

The algorithm is constantly being updated and tweaked in order to provide the best possible experience for users. This means that it is always changing and evolving, which can make it difficult for marketers to keep up. However, understanding how the algorithm works at its fundamental level has been essential for creating successful campaigns in Web 2.0.

Creating content can allow you to explore unique and niche topics while still making it available to the general public. It can also help in educating vast audiences. During the beginning of the worldwide pandemic in 2020, the Internet had a significant role in getting important information and updates to people around the world. Not only this, but our ability to communicate with our coworkers, continue sharing stuff with our friends, and stay in touch with family members, demonstrated that life may go on even in the midst of a global crisis.

CHAPTER 5

HOW THE GLOBAL PANDEMIC IMPACTED INTERNET USAGE

What made the Internet so revolutionary from the beginning was the fact that it made us so much more effective at communicating and doing business.

The new millennium saw a lot of advances in mobile devices which made the Internet even more accessible to more people. In the early 2000s, we had the introduction of 3G technology, which allowed for faster Internet speeds and more advanced features like video calling. This was a huge step forward for mobile devices, and it paved the way for even more advanced features in the years ahead. In 2007, Apple released the first iPhone which was a game-changer for the industry because it introduced new ways to interact with mobile devices for everything from your music collection, to the Internet. In much the same way that the iPhone changed the way we interacted with our mobile phones, the global pandemic changed the way we viewed and used the Internet.

In the years since the release of the iPhone, mobile devices have become more powerful, more capable, and more popular than ever before. This has created an all-new digital ecosystem as it's also the device where we most often access and browse the Internet. In recent years, the use of mobile phones to access the Internet has increased significantly due to a number of factors, including the increasing availability of high-speed mobile data networks and the number of tasks that we can now undertake online rather than in-person.

The global pandemic accelerated the transformation of the digital ecosystem and the digital economy, especially with regard to how much of our lives is spent online. The Internet has been transforming previously in-person activities for decades, but the pandemic only accelerated this trend.

Along came the global pandemic

The Coronavirus pandemic changed the way we use the Internet in a variety of ways. Perhaps most notably, it has led to a dramatic increase in the amount of time people are spending online.

Research conducted by GWI shows that, across all devices, the typical global Internet user in 2022 spends almost seven hours per day on the Internet.[1] Taking into consideration that the average person sleeps about seven to eight hours a night, typical Internet users are now spending more than 40 percent of their waking life online.[2] This time only seems to be growing, with the daily average increasing by four minutes per day over the past year. It may not sound like a big deal, however, if those four extra minutes per day are added up across all of the world's Internet users, it would amount to more than 5 billion additional days of Internet use in 2022.[3]

It's no surprise that social media usage skyrocketed during the pandemic. We all used these platforms to stay connected with those who we could no longer see in person. However, more significantly, people began turning to social media for news and information about the pandemic. This meant that in addition to providing entertainment and connection, social media had become a primary source of critical information and education.

By leveraging the powerful reach of social media, governments and health officials were able to quickly disseminate important updates and vital resources to where it was needed most. Social media as a result has moved from being a place just for fun and socialising into an essential tool for staying informed during times of crisis. It is clear that the impact of the global pandemic on social media usage will continue well beyond this period of upheaval, but the future is uncertain.

Social media has long been criticised for its negative effects on mental health, and the global pandemic has only exacerbated these concerns. For many, scrolling through Facebook or Instagram feeds was a constant source of stress during the pandemic. There was always something new to worry about, and constantly being exposed to updates and news stories about the pandemic was a recipe for anxiety.

Ultimately, the pandemic has illustrated just how powerful and influential social media can be. It has provided a platform for sharing stories, connecting with loved ones, and disseminating information – all of which are invaluable tools during times of uncertainty.

As we take steps towards restoring normalcy in our lives, it is essential that we continue to use social media responsibly and remain conscious of the potential risks associated with overusing these sites. By taking control of our online habits, we can also help ensure that social media remains a safe, trusted and positive space for everyone.

Contact tracing in the real world

With our lives increasingly moving online, we leave behind a trail of data that can be accessed, used and sold without our knowledge or consent. This raises serious concerns about our privacy and security, as well as the potential for fraud.

There are a number of steps that we can take to protect ourselves and our data, including using strong passwords and encrypting our communications, but ultimately it is up to the companies that hold our data and information to ensure that it is kept safe.

Unfortunately, the reality is that many of these companies have a bad reputation when it comes to protecting individuals' personal information. The past few years have seen a number of high-profile breaches in which sensitive information has been leaked or stolen. This has led to calls for greater regulation of the tech industry, with the goal of protecting our data from theft and misuse.

In the past, people were generally more trusting

of companies and institutions when it came to sharing their personal information. However, the pandemic has led to a marked increase in distrust, particularly when it comes to digital data.

According to an article posted by Harvard Business Review during the pandemic, a scorecard was used to determine how users feel about the digital trust environment. Out of 42 global economies on a 0-100 scale, an average score of 49 was given to the various mechanisms economies have in place to ensure safe and secure online ecosystems.[4] This level of mistrust is having a major impact on the way people share data online.

More and more people are now hesitating to share their personal information, even for basic tasks like creating an account or signing up for a service. This trend is likely to continue in the post-pandemic world, as people become more aware of the risks associated with sharing their data online.

Web 3.0 aims to address this by allowing users to have greater ownership over the personal data shared online. Companies like Google and Facebook are already introducing new features that give users more control and visibility over their data. Currently, this is done by allowing users to download a copy of their photos, messages, and posts. Additionally, both companies offer users the option of deleting data.

With these new features, Facebook and Google are demonstrating their commitment to giving users more control.

In the not-too-distant future, Internet users may be able to choose what information they share and who they share it with. It is also possible that they may be able to opt out of having their data collected at all if they wish. Ultimately, this shift will result in a more user-friendly and trusted online environment, which is essential for the continued growth of the World Wide Web.

CHAPTER 6

INTRODUCING WEB 3.0 (HERE'S WHAT WE KNOW)

Whenever Web 3.0 is mentioned, you can be forgiven for instantly thinking of NFT's, cryptocurrencies, blockchain and the Metaverse. It is true that these all play a part in what could be the overall landscape we expect in Web 3.0, however they each have their own role and purpose in how this new version of the Internet comes to life.

Web 3.0 is the third generation of the World Wide Web, where web pages are no longer just static documents, but instead are interactive experiences. The goal of Web 3.0 is to make the Internet more personal, social, and interactive than its predecessor.

The Internet in its original state, is the perfect example of a new technology that was reluctantly adopted and slowly embraced at the time. Many were quick to label it as a fad, simply a passing phase which would eventually lose popularity and interest. For these people, the tried and true methods of pre-Internet communication were immutable, and e-mails as well as instant online file sharing would never become the way of life for individuals, much less businesses.

In hindsight, it's easy to think that they should have recognised the opportunity that the Internet presented, but we should also understand that new technology like this at the time would have seemed entirely implausible and probably a bit unnecessary.

In the same way that Web 2.0 evolved, Web 3.0 is set to be another revolution in technology and in the way we interact online with brands and businesses.

The evolution that we are witnessing today, with a starting point that is oddly familiar to the early days of Web 1.0, indicates a steady progression toward a decentralised future. But what exactly does that mean?

The current Web 2.0 environment is reaching the late stages of its innovation curve. Desktop computers are being replaced by mobile devices and local storage is being replaced by cloud storage. We are fast evolving from the old ways of central, or fixed, systems and processes and quickly moving toward a more agile and distributed future. Simply put, this 'decentralised' future puts more capability and ownership back into the hands of the many, rather than the select few.

Centralisation vs decentralisation

The term 'centralised' refers to a system that is controlled and operated by one individual, a group of people or a corporate entity.

In Web 2.0, social media networks like Facebook and Instagram are examples of centralised systems because of the way in which the governing entity can exert its control over the system. This has been an issue for many years, particularly around the topics of censorship, freedom of speech, and data privacy, and it has become more and more prevalent in recent years.

Centralised social media platforms largely control the current marketing and advertising landscape. A rapid increase in online advertising has enabled these platforms to charge more over the years, but with minimal improvement in the benefits for brands or users.

Marketers are constantly at the mercy of the powerful corporations who they rely on to generate leads and revenue. If Facebook decides one day that the ads you have been running don't match their strict guidelines, then Facebook won't run those ads. There have been numerous stories of businesses who rely on social media networks like Facebook who have had their accounts shut down, sometimes for reasons unclear, which has resulted in major losses of income.

With a centralised system like Wikipedia, users can search millions of articles and get results based on their search criteria. In this instance, Wikipedia is the central server that holds all the articles from which users can then search.

One of the problems for centralised systems like this is that if the central server goes down, then so too does the ability to access that server. Thanks to blockchain technology, we finally have a way to satisfy the demand for platforms and systems that are decentralised, transparent and forever accessible.

By definition, blockchain is described as a way in which records are maintained across multiple computers linked in a peer-to-peer network. It's like having a 100% accurate, up-to-date ledger of transactions which every computer or participant on that network has a copy of. Meaning it can never go down, or be tampered with, and is completely validated by each peer in the network.

Blockchain technology creates a transparent web which increases consumer trust. This opens up a whole new world of possibilities, as it allows brands to break free from centralised marketing channels while being able to track accurate advertising expenditures in real time.

See you in the Metaverse

The Metaverse is a term that has taken on many meanings over the past few years, but all of them revolve in some way around virtual experience, online communities, and the creator economy.

There has already been a glimpse of how the Metaverse might begin to take shape and how decentralised web activity and virtual experiences might become a standard feature of Web 3.0 within the gaming and entertainment arena.

Even though Web 3.0 has always been associated with the Metaverse, every organisation should explore its potential to make headway in this emerging space.

Corporations like Meta (formerly Facebook) are seeking to be the pioneers in this market and have made large commercial investments into virtual and augmented reality providers.

Microsoft Mesh is a platform that enables users to connect and interact with each other in a shared, virtual, Metaverse space. Using avatars, users can communicate and collaborate with each other as if they were in the same physical space. Microsoft Mesh also allows users to share virtual objects, such as 3D models and documents. These objects can be viewed and manipulated by multiple users simultaneously, making it easier to work on projects together. In addition, Microsoft Mesh supports augmented reality, allowing users to see digital content superimposed over the real world. This makes it possible to view and interact with virtual objects as if they were real.

The platform is still in development, but it has the potential to change how we interact with each other and our surroundings. For example, imagine being able to attend a virtual concert with your friends, or explore a digital museum together. With these types of platforms, online experiences such as these are now in the realms of possibility. Many of the current Metaverse environments are based around the idea of creating a community. Readers will notice that this is a theme that repeats throughout the Internet, and it is a natural human desire to want to be a part of a community.

A bold, Internet-savvy type of consumer is emerging

As the world becomes more and more connected, it's no surprise that Generation Z – those born between 1996 and 2015 – are true digital natives. They are the first generation to grow up with the Internet as a part of their everyday lives, and this has had a profound effect on their attitudes and behaviours.

What sets Gen Z apart from previous generations is their comfort level with technology. For them, the Internet is not something new or scary – it's just a normal part of life. This is reflected in the way they use social media, which is often seen as a key characteristic of this generation.

According to a recent study, 58% of Gen Z can't go more than four hours without Internet access before they become uncomfortable. And it's not just social media – in 5 years, 64% of Gen Z thinks the Internet will determine what they will do on a daily basis.[1]

This comfort level with technology has led to some interesting behaviours. For example, there is a direct correlation between Gen Z's digital habits and their physical preferences, with 75% of Gen Z more likely to buy a product if they can customise it, compared to 56% of Baby Boomers. Additionally, 41% of Gen Z – more than any other generation – said that they will forgo security/privacy concerns and provide their data so long as they receive a personalised experience in return.[2]

Of course, this isn't to say that all Gen Z'ers are tech-savvy, Internet-loving consumers. But it does show that this generation is comfortable with technology and is willing to use it in creative ways. This suggests that they will continue to be early adopters of new technology and will find new and innovative ways to use it in their lives. This comfort level with technology also has implications for the workplace. As more and more jobs require technical skills, those who are comfortable with technology will have a clear advantage.

In 2023, platforms like Discord, Telegram, and Medium present some of the biggest opportunities for brands to become established in front of Gen Z and current Web 3.0 communities.

The decentralised and permissionless nature of these platforms makes them an attractive alternative to Web 2.0 social media networks for brands and businesses hoping to begin building audiences ahead of the current Internet evolution.

As a result of changing global attitudes toward how we use the Internet and create and consume content, we're now seeing an entirely new creator economy rise around content production as a viable job alternative and source of income.

When the global pandemic came along, people started to see work in a new way. Work used to be more-or-less something you did for a paycheck, but now more and more people want to do work that is fulfilling and meaningful. They want to use their skills and talents to create something they're passionate about, rather than simply earn an income.

Another reason for the growth of the creator economy is that technology has made it easier for people to create things on their own. With the Internet and tools like Photoshop and Illustrator, anyone can create something amazing without having to go through a traditional publishing or manufacturing process. Online programs like Canva have taken it even further by creating a comprehensive graphic design software that can easily be used by someone without any prior experience in design.

The creator economy represents the growing online economic activity around content creators and their ability to generate revenue from their followers and fans. This includes activities such as selling products, services or advertising, charging for access to content, or using platforms to connect with larger audiences.

CHAPTER 7

PROFITING IN THE CREATOR ECONOMY

The rise of the creator economy has been one of the most exciting things to watch in the marketing world. It's a trend that has been years in the making, and one which is only going to continue to further develop and expand alongside Web 3.0 in the years to come.

In what could also be referred to as the 'consumer economy', this lucrative new way of making money is being driven by creators who are able to monetise their skills, abilities and content creations almost exclusively online. This can include everyone from bloggers and vloggers, to social media influencers and more. The content production and distribution platforms they use, as well as the very tools that allow creators to monetise their content, are constantly developing new ways of streamlining processes that allow these creators to capitalise.

The creator economy is set to grow exponentially with Web 3.0 and we're only just now seeing a glimpse into what the future might hold.

One of the main driving factors of this new economy is the increasing rate of content consumption. When we consume content online, we are fuelling the overall creator economy whether we subscribe to our favourite creator or not, because of the data that's being shared. This isn't necessarily a bad thing – after all, it's the data that allows platforms to personalise our experience and show us content that we're more likely to enjoy.

Looking back in the years leading up to 2020, content marketing was the primary way in which businesses could reach and define new audiences. The content being created was mainly for audience building purposes or otherwise to boost a site's ability to be found on Google via SEO. However, what we are seeing now is a growing emphasis placed on the quality of the content rather than the quantity of content produced.

As such, there is now a major shift toward ways in which the creators themselves are incentivised for their content. Just like it did in the evolution from Web 1.0 to Web 2.0, this whole new landscape has the ability to completely change the way we think about scalable, online content marketing. It even has the potential to create entirely new revenue streams for businesses, simply by the way they market their brand or business and the content they produce online.

Social media has made it increasingly easier for creators to connect with audiences, share content and all the while get paid for doing so. With the Internet becoming ever more accessible, and social media platforms refining their data-based algorithms, the creator economy is exploding.

There are now countless content creators

across a wide range of industries who are finding new ways to monetise their content and create sustainable online businesses.

Content creators reaching new heights

Mr Beast is a famous content creator who has gained a huge following on YouTube, earning around $30 million per year from his videos.[1] He is known for his creative and often outrageous videos which has earned him over 10 million subscribers and billions of views, and is one of the most successful YouTubers of all time.

Mr Beast, real name Jimmy Donaldson, first rose to fame with his unique brand of challenge videos, which saw him undertake crazy stunts in order to win money or prizes.

His unique content and willingness to push the boundaries has made him a favourite with viewers around the world, amassing millions of views within days. Since Mr Beast started, he has given away millions of dollars to strangers, donated huge sums of money to charity and even bought an entire island.

Aside from his YouTube channel which has over 40 million subscribers, Mr Beast also has a successful merchandise line and a range of other businesses, and is estimated to be worth around $25 million making him one of the richest YouTubers in the world.[2] It was even recently revealed that Mr Beast received a $1 billion offer in 2022 to sell his channel, so it seems that there are those with billions of dollars to spend who are confident in the future of content creation.

The key players in the creator economy are the content creators themselves, along with the platforms and companies that enable them to reach large audiences. For example, YouTube provides a platform for creators to upload and share videos, while also offering tools for monetisation.

Similarly, Patreon is an online tool which allows creators to set up membership tiers and collect monthly payments from their fans and followers.

The benefits of the creator economy are twofold. First, it provides new opportunities for everyday people to make a living from their creativity. Second, it helps to support the creation of high-quality content by giving creators an incentive to produce material that their audience will value. Brands and businesses need only then align themselves with the right content creator in order to reach greater audiences and generate more quality leads.

In the past, it was difficult for creators to monetise their content unless they had a large following. Even still, platform providers often take a large percentage of the revenue generated by creators, which eats into their earnings. Redargless, platforms like Instagram and YouTube are continually coming up with ways to help creators monetise their networks, while providing a seamless user experience that delivers relevant content directly to the users feed.

Users can even now pay a small recurring fee to subscribe to their favourite content creator which allows them to access exclusive content, subscriber-only group chats and a range of other benefits such as discount codes on products or merchandise. This is a huge opportunity for the creators themselves who have built up a loyal following on these channels, as they can now generate regular revenue and income from their content and following.

Additionally, fans who subscribe can also receive exclusive emojis and badges to signify their subscription level and differentiate themselves among other users.

Instagram has been one of the pioneers in enabling a more cohesive e-commerce and social media experience by launching a new feature which allows users to instantly link out to products seen in images. These shoppable posts allow users to conveniently purchase directly from their social media feed. With these features, it's clear that Instagram is serious about becoming a hub for creators and users to connect and do business.

The creator economy in the near future may be intricately linked with how everyday users and content creators generate income online. Blockchain for example has permitted a safe and secure platform for users to be rewarded for what they do online in a completely traceable manner, facilitating more valuable interactions and the generation of income in the form of cryptocurrency and digital assets.

A cryptocurrency for your thoughts

For the creator economy to continue to thrive, creators need to be paid for what they do.

Whether it's an affiliation or brand sponsorship, or direct advertising of a product or service, for creators to be rewarded for the content they produce means that a transaction has to take place.

Much is the same for all the economies which we are familiar with today. Over the last decade, cryptocurrencies have been making their way into our lives as a form of digital rewards and online currency. Although many are still yet to fully grasp the vast potential of an online reward system, digital currencies are currently experiencing a surge in popularity with many businesses now gearing up to ride the wave.

Cryptocurrencies by definition are a range of digital or virtual currencies that use cryptography for security, making them extremely difficult to counterfeit. Cryptocurrencies are characterised by their organic and decentralised nature; meaning they are not issued by any central authority, rendering them theoretically immune to manipulation or interference.

The most prevalent cryptocurrency, and also the oldest, is Bitcoin. Instant payments are enabled by Bitcoin's decentralised peer-to-peer technology which was created by an anonymous person or group of people with the nickname Satoshi Nakamoto in or around 2009. Bitcoin is largely thought of as the first and primary cryptocurrency. There are currently more than 19 million Bitcoins in circulation, with a total market value of over $300 billion as of January 2023.[3]

The adoption of decentralised cryptocurrencies around the world has been steadily growing. Numerous Central Banks of nations around the world are also exploring the use of cryptocurrency as a central bank digital currency (CBDC), so it is clear that many are taking the future of this seriously.

For the Web of the future to function effectively, we need to rethink online payment systems as well as rewards for sharing our data online. With Bitcoin and other cryptocurrencies, we may be close to such a system as they not only enable instantaneous and borderless transactions at extremely low fees, but also have the ability to 'pay' users of the blockchain as a reward for a range of online activities. All of which is completely and transparently recorded on the blockchain ledger.

Tokens as digital assets

The rise of non-fungible tokens, or NFTs, has been one of the most talked-about topics in the cryptocurrency/marketing space over the past year. NFTs are digital assets that are unique and cannot be replaced by another identical asset. A fungible token, on the other hand, is interchangeable and can be replaced with another identical token; unlike fiat currencies such as the dollar, or certain cryptocurrencies like Bitcoin.

Arguably, one of the most popular uses for NFTs so far has been in the gaming industry, where they have been used to represent virtual items such as in-game currency, and even game characters. However, the potential applications for NFTs go far beyond gaming.

NFTs are unique, so each has a different value. Digital assets such as artwork, music, or other forms of digital content can be represented using NFTs. They can also serve as a means for things like customer rewards or loyalty points. In some cases, NFTs may even include physical assets such as real estate, resources and commodities, or even rare artwork.

One of the great things about NFTs is that they offer a new way for creators to monetise their work. For example, an artist could potentially sell an NFT version of their artwork for a much higher price than they could sell the physical artwork. This is because the NFT represents a unique piece of digital content that can be bought and sold like any other asset.

NFTs have already been used to sell a wide range of items, from artwork and music, to collectables and are even now being used to sell famous viral videos and Internet 'memes'.

As the popularity of cryptocurrencies and NFTs continues to grow, we are likely to see more and more innovative applications for them. So far, they have proven to be a very exciting and versatile new technology with a lot of potential.

The creator economy is rapidly changing what the Internet means to everyday people. This is bringing about a renaissance in creativity as businesses look to new ways to market their brands and engage with customers. Along with new technologies that enable cross-border transactions and the use of digital assets, we can foresee a revolution ahead of us that looks sure to make a huge impact in our daily lives.

CHAPTER 8

THE RENAISSANCE OF MARKETING: A NEW ERA DAWNS

The marketing revolution that is currently underway marks a shift from traditional, linear marketing models to more modern, customer-centric approaches.

This new way of thinking about marketing puts the customer at the centre of the decision-making process and emphasises engagement and relationships over transactions.

While we still don't know exactly what will define the Web 3.0 world, there are many hallmark traits that we are already experiencing. This includes AI-driven services, blockchain infrastructure, and decentralised data architecture. For this reason, Web 3.0 is sometimes also referred to as the Semantic Web, or the Global Brain because of the integrated and smart nature of its implementation.

It is highly likely that the evolution currently underway won't be fully realised until years into the future as we are only now just learning about new virtual technologies that aim to enhance the way we communicate and integrate with the online world.

The rise of interconnected technology is a major force behind the marketing revolution. Customers are now more connected than ever before, thanks to mobile devices and social media. This has given them more power in the marketplace and increased their ability to research and compare products and services.

As a result, businesses must now focus on providing a personalised, relevant, and engaging customer experience in order to stay ahead of the competition. This is leading to a renaissance of data-driven marketing and forces brands to revisit the basics which seem to have been forgotten in recent years.

The future of marketing is in the hands of the consumer

In a world where customers are empowered with information and can easily connect with one another to share opinions, reviews and ideas, businesses must adapt their marketing strategies to remain relevant.

The challenge that many businesses currently face when developing marketing strategies is to continually create enough relevant content that is engaging and resonates with customers, while at the same time helping them to make informed purchasing decisions.

In the past, businesses controlled the flow of information and could dictate what customers should know about their products or services. However, with the rise of social media and other online platforms, customers now have a much louder voice and can easily connect with one another to share their experiences and opinions about brands, products, and services. As a result, businesses can no longer completely control the message; they must now focus instead on differentiating themselves through the use of their brand and going further to provide a positive experience to customers. By doing so, businesses can build a profile with customers and create a loyal online following. In the end, it's the customer who will determine the success or failure of a business; therefore, marketing strategies must be designed with the customer in mind.

To date, brands and businesses have relied on their digital marketing efforts to bridge the gap between building awareness and highlighting their product or service. Marketers are constantly having to showcase ROI to business owners and stakeholders that the marketing budget is being spent appropriately, or is achieving the predetermined purpose. However, as marketers know, not all leads or enquiries received will directly translate into sales or profits.

There are always going to be those that don't quite match the criteria or in one way or another do not result in becoming a customer. There is also the potential that your ads might not even be seen altogether thanks to Ad Blockers. But, what if there was a way that your advertising budget could be spent knowing for a fact that your ads will be viewed by the right audience and those most likely to become a potential customer?

Pay-to-play advertising

Have you ever been paid to watch an advertisement? It may seem like a silly question, but it's one that is becoming more of a reality as digital tokens become more popular.

While most people are familiar with Bitcoin, Ethereum, and other major cryptocurrencies, there are thousands of other digital tokens that are being used for a variety of purposes. Some of these tokens are being used to pay people for their attention.

Traditionally, companies in the past might have paid people with vouchers or discounts to participate in marketing research campaigns. However, these programs were often difficult to track and manage. With digital tokens, it is possible to create a system that is transparent and easy to track.

There are a number of companies already working on this concept. Basic Attention Token, for example, is a digital token that is meant to be used to pay people for their attention.

The company behind the token, Brave, has created a browser that allows users to opt-in to viewing ads. When a user views an ad, they are paid in Basic Attention Tokens.

This system provides a number of benefits for both advertisers and users. Advertisers can be sure that their ads are being seen by people who are very likely to be interested in them. Users, on the other hand, can be paid for their attention without having to worry about providing personal information against their will or watching irrelevant ads.

In the future, brands might enhance these experiences by rewarding users for answering direct questions or sharing personal data that helps marketers gain a better understanding of their evolving customer needs.

The purpose of advertising campaigns in the future might be more for brand awareness building rather than for direct sales. Marketers therefore will need to be smart with how they engage with consumers and might have to rely on the attention token system to reward people for engaging with their ad.

This may sound counter-intuitive, but it actually opens up incredible opportunities to create positive and lifelong relationships with customers. Take for example a woman who opts in to view an advertisement from Brand A. She agrees to be rewarded up to five digital tokens for her participation, which will be transferred directly to her secure online wallet in the form of 'Brand A Coin'. After she enters her name, postcode and e-mail, two brief questions pop up on screen which she answers before watching a short video. Once the video ends another two questions are asked, this time the questions are a little more in-depth, so she completes the first but skips the final question. In this scenario, the woman was rewarded with four Brand A Coins because she provided answers to a total of three questions and watched more than 90% of the video. The tokens that she has accumulated can now be used on Brand A's online store as credit or as payment to access exclusive products, discounts or promotions.

The entire interaction might only last seconds or minutes, but is almost guaranteed to have a lasting impact on both the consumer and the marketer that's advertising Brand A.

Television advertising is not dead

We are living in a short-attention-span society and businesses already have to work hard to attract and engage consumers. Pay-to-play advertising is a great way for businesses to bridge the ever-widening gap between marketing spend and return on investment.

Up until recently, the pinnacle of advertising was

having the right 30-second ad slot during high-viewership prime-time TV. Despite the lack of measurable ROI, and a largely "pay and pray" approach, every business wanted to get their brand on TV because of the amount of people it could reach, along with the perceived value it would bring to the brand.

Thanks to streaming technology, companies are now able to form a direct relationship with consumers by having their content readily available online, conveniently housed within a user-friendly and intuitive app.

Streaming services offer us our favourite TV shows and content at the touch of a button, and can even make recommendations of programs and content we will enjoy based on what we've already watched.

One of the major streaming services, Hulu, now enables the opportunity for businesses of all sizes to advertise on their platform, offering a cost-effective way of reaching a large and engaged audience. This means that if you're a Hulu subscriber on an ad-supported plan, you will see ads during your shows and films, typically at the start of the stream and placed throughout the video. This is similar to what you would experience on traditional TV programming; but this time, and for as little as $500, a local brand can potentially be seen directly after a big brand.

This brings huge credibility to local brands and small businesses that they would have only dreamed of with traditional TV methods. Advertisers also have the added ability to see campaigns in real-time, breaking down the number of impressions by device type and even content genre.

Logging into your advertising dashboard on Hulu will give you an instant overview of your advertising performance, something which linear TV campaigns have not been able to do.

Since the global pandemic, greater numbers of consumers have gravitated toward streaming services for entertainment and content, in line with longer times spent online and increased mobile device usage. This form of entertainment at our fingertips is bringing about an evolution in app integration in our daily lives and it's leaving marketers struggling to keep up, but regardless of how many things continue to evolve or change in the marketing world, one factor remains the same – the brand.

The brand identity of a business is already essential but is becoming increasingly more so leading into the new Web 3.0 world across an increasing number of different touchpoints.

Branding has always been of utmost importance as it directly relates to how that business or service is perceived. Changing brand perception is probably one of the most difficult things a company can do. This is because the perception is not owned by the company – it's owned by its customers. First impressions count too, in fact, it takes a reported 0.05 seconds for a customer to form an opinion, good or bad, upon landing on a website for the first time.[1]

Every single touchpoint someone has with a business has a similar effect, and a strong, well-designed brand not only underpins the experience, but can also instantly instill trust with those who are experiencing it. For this reason, every business and marketer needs to ensure that their brand is set on strong foundations.

For many, this means coming back to the basics of branding to be able to better anticipate ways to move ahead in Web 3.0.

CHAPTER 9

MASTER THE BRAND BASICS FOR SURVIVAL

When it comes to branding, it's not just what you say, but also what you do that matters. You can attract new customers, increase customer loyalty, and increase profitability all by building a strong brand.

In the marketplace of the future, an effective brand will be essential for any business that wants to succeed. Brand is what sets you apart from your competitors and helps you to connect with your target audience. It's what makes you recognisable, and it's one of the most important aspects of any successful business.

In visual terms, a brand is the combination of a name, logo, and set of distinctive colours and fonts that are used to identify a product or company. Branding is more than just the visual representation of the business, it's also the association that people have with the product, service, or company.

For example, when you think of Nike, you might think of athleticism and success. When you think of McDonald's, you might think of fast food and happy memories.

Creating a strong brand takes time and effort, but it's worth it in the long run. A brand should be an accurate representation of the business, the values that it stands for, and should be reflective of the quality of the products or services, and the overall customer experience, that the brand offers.

Most importantly, it should be consistent. In fact, one report found that consistent branding can increase business revenue by up to 20%.[1] Building a consistent brand isn't easy, but it's essential for any business that wants to succeed in the long term, and investing in branding early on will pay off down the road as the business grows and gains more customers.

Branding has become increasingly important in the modern marketplace as customers have become more savvy and less loyal.

In order to compete, businesses need to create a strong brand identity that resonates with potential customers. This can be accomplished in a number of ways, but one of the most effective is to showcase the values of the brand through its actions and tonality.

For example, a brand that values environmental sustainability might choose to use recycled materials in its packaging or partner with eco-friendly suppliers. Similarly, a brand that focuses on social responsibility might donate a portion of its profits to charity or engage in cause campaigns.

By aligning actions with values, a brand can create a powerful sense of identity that can attract new customers and build loyalty among existing ones. Taking a stand on issues that matter to your customers and remaining consistent in your messaging, can show the world what your brand is all about. Furthermore, by staying true to your values, you can ensure that your marketing efforts will have a lasting impact.

Steve Jobs, co-founder of Apple, is widely recognised as a pioneer in both the computer industry and the marketing of consumer electronics. His work in these fields has had a profound impact on the way we live and work, and also the way we see brands today. He believed that at its core, marketing is about values and what a customer feels when they interact with a brand.

Jobs argues that businesses must first create value for their customers, and then communicate that value through marketing efforts. How they retain those customers then comes down to their experience and what they felt before, during and after their interaction. This, he believed, is the only way to build a lasting relationship and create truly loyal customers.

Apple as a brand believed that there are people in this world that could change it for the better, and that those people, who are crazy enough to think that they can, are the ones that actually do. This was their core value and the foundation of the infamous Think Different campaign, which in many ways is still at the heart of the Apple brand today. Steve Jobs was a visionary leader and his insistence on core brand values has inspired generations of marketers.

In the Web 3.0 environment, businesses must ensure that their own core values as a brand are set on strong foundations. Values that are consistent with the overall purpose of the business are one of the most effective ways of showing customers that your actions speak louder than words. This will lead to greater consumer trust and opens the door to so many marketing campaign possibilities.

Back to brand basics

While the concept of branding is centuries old, the term “brand” was first coined in the 1800s by cattle ranchers who burned brands into their cattle’s flesh to indicate ownership.

In the late 19th century, as trade expanded and producers began targeting specific markets, factories began engraving brands onto their products.

Branding in the modern era has become increasingly complex, with companies spending millions of dollars on research and development to create brand identities that resonate with consumers. Over time, various metrics have been developed to measure the success of a brand which fall under three key pillars; brand equity, brand awareness, and brand loyalty.

These are the basic factors that any business or marketer must master in order to ensure their brand remains in the minds and hearts of consumers long into the future.

Just as Steve Jobs recognised the importance of getting back to Apple's core purpose and value, brands in 2023 and beyond must recognise the basics of a successful brand in order to strengthen their foundations.

Brand Basic #1: *Equity*

When it comes to brand equity, businesses must make sure that they are creating a positive image that consumers can relate to.

It's no secret that businesses with strong, positive brand equity tend to perform better than those without. After all, customers are more likely to purchase products and services from companies they trust and feel good about, so the sentiment surrounding a brand must be kept positive to ensure the brand equity remains high.

This can be done by ensuring that all touchpoints with the customer are positive experiences, including everything from the way a customer is greeted at a store to the packaging of products. Ultimately, whatever values the brand lives by, must be evident in everything that the business does. When customers see that your brand cares about more than just making money, they'll be more likely to develop positive feelings towards it. Additionally, positive brand equity can also lead to improved staff morale and increased employee productivity.

Investing in brand equity is an investment in the business' most important asset – people. By creating a strong, positive brand, you can build a foundation for success that will pay dividends for years to come.

Brand Basic #2: ***Awareness***

Consumer awareness of a brand refers to how familiar they are with its products and services. In many cases, it is determined by how many consumers can correctly name or identify a brand after being presented with the logo.

Awareness of the brand is often the first step in the consumer decision-making process and is therefore essential for businesses that want to increase sales and market share.

As the key driver of purchase intent, brand awareness plays a pivotal role in the consumer decision-making process. It can also have a direct impact on the amount that a consumer spends. When comparing similar products online, 4,000 U.S. consumers were asked to identify the factors that led them to choose the more expensive option. The results showed that 46% of those surveyed admitted that they pay more for a brand that they trust.[2]

There are a number of ways to increase brand awareness, including advertising, public relations, and word-of-mouth marketing.

Advertising is the most direct way to increase brand awareness. It allows businesses to reach a large audience with their message and helps create a lasting impression in the minds of consumers. Public relations can also be used to raise brand awareness, through activities such as media relations, event marketing, and thought leadership. Word-of-mouth marketing is another effective way to increase brand awareness, as it relies on customer recommendations to generate interest and excitement about a product or service.

Brand Basic #3: ***Loyalty***

Finally, brand loyalty is what will keep customers coming back to a business time and time again.

To create loyalty, businesses need to provide an exceptional customer experience that makes the individual feel valued. When customers feel valued, they are more likely to continue spending with that brand and recommend it to their family and friends.

Customers that are “loyal” to the brand are typically more valuable because they are less likely to switch to a competitor, even if there is a price difference. This can lead to greater market share in addition to increased profit. For consumers, being loyal to a brand can mean receiving discounts, rewards, and special treatment. However, offering too many discounts or rewards can devalue the program and turn off potential customers.

Instead, businesses should focus on creating a well-rounded loyalty program that offers a variety of benefits to both new and loyal customers that promotes a lifelong relationship.

Brand equity, brand awareness, and brand loyalty are three of the most important factors that businesses need to focus on in order to remain relevant and top of mind to consumers. By creating a positive image, increasing brand awareness, and providing an exceptional customer experience, businesses will be able to build a loyal customer base that keeps coming back time and again.

Thanks to Web 3.0 technology, providing memorable brand experiences are coming to life in new and exciting ways. Experience marketing is fast becoming a key strategy of a marketers toolkit because of the way it can impact an individual as a happy memory or an experience which they can share with their friends and families, as well as the potential to involve their spheres of influence.

CHAPTER 10

CREATING UNFORGETTABLE CUSTOMER EXPERIENCES

Experience marketing is a relatively new technique that emphasises customer experience above all else, and is already changing the way businesses think about their marketing strategy.

In the past, businesses have focused on creating advertising and promotions that reach as many people as possible in the shortest time. The idea behind this would be that the more people who saw the ad, the more likely it was that some of them would become customers. With experience marketing, the focus is shifted to creating an amazing individual customer experience that will keep people coming back for more, while also positively recommending their friends and network. To do this, businesses need to put critical thought into their customer service, their product offerings, and their overall brand image in the marketplace. It also means that brands need to find new ways to appeal to customers' emotions and build lifelong relationships with them.

Benefits for brands include improved customer satisfaction, higher customer loyalty, and increased word-of-mouth marketing. In addition, experience marketing can help build a stronger brand identity which can help to further differentiate the brand from its competitors.

When done well, experience marketing can be an extremely powerful tool for businesses. However, it's important to ensure that all touchpoints are considered and that the brand is able to deliver on its promises. Otherwise, the result can be negative experiences that damages reputation. Current experience marketing tactics can include everything from interactive displays and marketing gamification, to immersive and exclusive events. These types of experiences are especially beneficial when they aim to help consumers understand how the product works, or highlighting benefits the business can offer, all the while showcasing the overall experience of belonging to that brand.

Hosting events in the Metaverse

In the Metaverse, brands can offer experiences that are unrepeatable in real life, as well as being able to reimagine spaces and experiences from the real world.

There are a few different ways that businesses can host events in the Metaverse. One way is to create a space within a virtual world for people to gather and interact.

This could be something as simple as renting out a plot of land within an already established virtual world, or it could be more complex, such as creating a custom-built environment that mimics a specific real world venue. Another option is to use one of the many event-related platforms that have been developed specifically for the Metaverse. These platforms provide everything from basic chat and voice features to more sophisticated tools for managing avatar interactions and multimedia content in a range of different environments.

In 2020, online gaming platform Roblox hosted one of the first virtual concerts which was held over two days exclusively within the Roblox virtual gaming world. This followed a similar event in another virtual game world, Fortnite, where popular music industry artist Travis Scott hosted an in-game concert that attracted over 12 million concurrent players at its peak.[1]

Roblox is unique because players can create their own virtual worlds within the game and play in a variety of different game types.

Similarly to Minecraft, players can build their own maps and game modes, and then share them with the community. Additionally, through the use of a virtual in-game currency called Robux, the platform offers users the ability to purchase in-game items, enhance game experiences, customise a player's avatar, or acquire development resources. In recent months, Roblox has become increasingly popular for hosting virtual concerts featuring some of the biggest names in the music industry, including Justin Bieber, Marshmello, and Imagine Dragons.

During the pandemic, iconic fashion brand Gucci partnered with Roblox to recreate a virtual version of their real-life exhibition on show in Florence to mark the brand's 100th anniversary.

The event was called "Gucci Garden" and featured a Gucci Store, Gucci Museum, and a Gucci Restaurant, and was visited by over 20 million people during the two-week period.[2] In the virtual Gucci world, players were able to transform their avatars into mannequins that allowed them to try on different Gucci virtual items that were available to purchase. Notably, a Queen Bee Dionysus bag sold for $4,115, which was over $1,000 more than the original price tag of the real-life, physical bag.[3] The Gucci Garden virtual experience was a one-of-a-kind event that blended fashion, entertainment, and gaming in an innovative way.

Gamifying the marketing experience

Gamification is the process of using game or competition tactics and thinking in non-game contexts in order to engage users, solve problems and encourage desired behaviours. In marketing, gamification can be used to increase customer engagement, loyalty and conversions, as well as helping to collect data and insights about customer behaviour.

There are a number of ways businesses can gamify their marketing efforts in order to encourage more engagement from customers. Methods of gamification in marketing include providing rewards for certain actions, such as points, badges, or leaderboard positions.

Badges are one of the most common forms of gamification and are often used to encourage users to perform certain actions or to reward consumers for their loyalty. For example, Foursquare awards users with badges for checking into different locations, and Airbnb gives hosts a badge and 'Superhost' status when they achieve consistently good reviews.

By aligning these incentives with company goals, businesses can create powerful motivation for consumers to take the desired actions.

Companies have been using gamification in marketing long before the term was coined. Over the years, Coca-Cola has run many successful campaigns and promotions using gamification. Some promotions required participants to collect special bottle caps, which they would have to stick to a printed saver sheet.[4] Those who collected the caps could send the completed sheet back to Coca-Cola to win a prize, although some people were happy by simply collecting the whole set and putting them in a saver sheet, satisfied that they had completed the challenge.

More recently, McDonald's has used games as a way to drive sales with their hugely popular Monopoly promotion and is one of the best examples of successful gamification in action.

A variety of gamification techniques are employed in McDonald's Monopoly to provide customers with an enjoyable, alluring experience and is a customer favourite because it's so easy to play. Buy any menu item and you'll get game pieces that can be redeemed for prizes like merchandise vouchers, discounts on future McDonald's purchases or even cars. The promotion has been hugely successful for years because it requires little to no effort beyond buying food from McDonald's.

Customers don't have to enter codes or remember to check back after a certain date for winners, they just receive their prize along with their order. This game is similar to scratch cards in both the game pieces and the peel-to-reveal mechanism. Moreover, the entire promotion revolves around one of history's most beloved board games. McDonald's is a popular place to eat, regardless of whether they are running a Monopoly promotion. Gamifying the experience further by offering more game pieces with more expensive menu items has proved to be a great way to upsell their customers.

In recent years, McDonald's has stayed on top of consumer trends by digitalising the popular Monopoly promotion without losing the excitement that the physical tickets bring to their customers. To achieve this, McDonald's created an online virtual game board accessed through an app. However, they also had to combat the growing perception that winning anything beyond low-value prizes was nearly impossible. Through a phased strategy, McDonald's first created awareness of the upcoming campaign, before delivering the message of "1 in 5 Wins Instantly" which was seen across YouTube, paid search, Twitter, mobile display ads, and more.[5]

Originally McDonald's focused on displaying the prizes that could be won through the app. After that, it targeted its audiences with evidence of people who were winning in their area. As ad fatigue started to take effect, McDonald's employed a re-engagement strategy to bring users back into the app, by offering more games that could be played to increase guest count in restaurants.

Near the end of the campaign, to further boost sales, McDonald's promoted content and ads around how many prizes were still up for grabs. This helped spike app usage during the final weeks. The digitalisation of the campaign was such a success that the app was still being used by half of all players two weeks after they downloaded it, and it was still being used by over a third of users six weeks later.[6]

As a result of the mobile app, people were able to play the game in a completely new way, with the addition of the virtual game board that improved visibility of the prizes on offer and eliminated the necessity of retaining paper tickets. It also allowed customers to see who was currently winning prizes near them in real time.

Gamification can be particularly effective in digital marketing campaigns, where it can be used to drive participation in activities. Additionally, by incorporating game elements into website design or mobile apps, businesses can make their online experiences more engaging and addictive, leading to increased customer loyalty. Gamification is not limited to only marketing, it can also be used as a powerful tool for brands to tell their story and create memorable experiences.

Exploring new computer-enhanced realities

As we become more accustomed to technology being a part of our everyday lives, it's no surprise that augmented reality (AR) is becoming more commonplace as well.

What was once considered a futuristic concept is now rapidly becoming reality, with AR glasses and contact lenses already in development. Augmented reality has enormous potential and is already being utilised by businesses and is rapidly changing the way we view the world and it is starting to be used extensively in an increasing amount of ways.

We see this all the time on apps like Snapchat and Instagram with face filters, as well as gaming apps like Pokemon Go, augmented reality continues to change the way we interact with the real world. Art galleries are taking AR even further by offering visitors interactive experiences in place of previous self-guided tours.

The Louvre in Paris decided to explore the possibilities by offering visitors dual-touchscreen tour devices. These portable platforms come complete with a fully interactive navigation system that lets users program their own trajectory through the labyrinthine museum. With more than 600 photos, 30+ hours of audio commentary, 3D interactive models, interviews and trivia, these handheld devices become visitors' personal guides to one of the world's most famous museums.[7]

So much content is available on these devices that their maker, Nintendo, released the program as a stand-alone game. Anyone with a Nintendo DS can gain access to hundreds of years of art and history from the Louvre, even if they never intend to physically visit for themselves. Enhancing the experience further are Bluetooth beacons placed throughout the museum which track the users movement to show content relevant to each location.

There are now platforms, such as Eyejack and Artivive, which can use a smartphone's camera to identify 'markers' and activate a superimposed video or animation overlay in real time.

This means that any uniquely identifiable image can be used as a canvas for creation, making paintings the perfect candidate. So, all you Harry Potter fans out there can rejoice because we've taken a real step toward paintings that can now come to life before your eyes!

With its ability to superimpose digital information onto the real world, AR has huge potential to change the way we live and work. It's estimated that by 2025, the global AR market will be worth over US$198 billion.[8] This rapid growth is driven by a number of factors, including the increasing popularity of AR gaming and entertainment, as well as the growing use of AR in enterprise applications such as training and product visualisation. Mobile technology and integrated devices are making it easier for everyday people to access the excitement and delights of augmented reality.

Technology has definitely come a long way and greater innovation is only around the corner. As we saw with Web 2.0, the gradual progression toward new technological understandings lead to the seemingly rapid adoption of social media and online content sharing.

As the Web 3.0 era unfolds, we can expect to see more and more innovative ways of enhancing the consumer experience.

This will be first to benefit the brands and businesses who are making tangible steps today to provide an outstanding online experience for customers tomorrow.

CHAPTER 11

THE FUTURE AND THE MARKETERS IN IT

The future is approaching at astonishing speed and we are already in the midst of unfathomable change.

Technology is continuing to develop at an exponential rate and companies are only just starting to understand now the power and potential of Web 3.0. Things that were once thought to be stuff of science fiction are now facts of life.

This is an entirely new era, where technology enables us to do things that we never thought possible. Brands, businesses and marketers alike need to ensure that they are prepared for the future and position themselves accordingly to be able to make the most of the opportunities that it will surely bring. This is why it is so important for brands to stay ahead of the curve and keep up with the latest trends to be able to foresee what changes that Web 3.0 will inevitably bring to the marketing sphere.

One of the biggest changes we are seeing in marketing is the rise of artificial intelligence (AI). One of the most transformative technologies of our time, AI has the power to enable businesses to automate and scale many marketing tasks, including customer segmentation, content creation, and lead generation. Not only that, but it also can be extremely beneficial in a variety of advertising applications such as personalising communications by analysing past behaviour and providing insights into what each lead is interested in and what type of content is most likely to resonate with them.

This information can then be used to create targeted content that is more likely to result in a conversion. Although Artificial Intelligence in marketing is still in its early developmental stages, there are many current opportunities to explore and experiment with that are already available to utilise.

However, businesses should start small when it comes to implementing AI into their marketing strategy and pick one specific use case that could have a measurable impact, and then focus on getting that right before moving on to other uses. Let's dive in.

Using AI to refine lead generation processes

AI already has the ability to automate a number of tasks that were once done manually, and can make a wide range of marketing processes more accurate and effective.

For example, AI lead generation software uses specific algorithms to scrape data from the web and automatically identify and contact potential leads from various online sources, such as social media, websites, and forums. This data can then be analysed to identify potential leads, scoring them based on their likelihood of becoming customers.

This scoring can help sales teams prioritise which leads to follow up with first and is an invaluable tool for businesses that want to generate more quality leads and improve their conversion rates. However, it is important to note that it is not a silver bullet; it will not automatically generate sales or guarantee results. Rather, it can simply help businesses to more efficiently and effectively identify and contact potential leads at the right time, which can ultimately lead to more sales and greater return on advertising spend.

The future of sentiment analysis in marketing

Sentiment analysis refers to gathering customer sentiment from online reviews, social media comments, and other various written media that can be analysed to determine the overall feeling or pulse of an audience or network. The applications for this technology are vast, and range from customer service to political polling.

As businesses strive to provide the best customer experience possible, more and more are turning to AI algorithms to help streamline the process and identify customer sentiment and opportunities for improvement before they become an issue.

By understanding how customers feel about their products and services, businesses can make necessary changes to improve the customer experience and avoid any negative repercussions.

The benefits are widespread such as targeting marketing campaigns to specific audiences and quickly assessing how effective a product is once it's released to the market. For example, an AI algorithm could be used to identify negative sentiment in real time which can allow the brand or business to take the steps necessary to address the issue head-on.

Additionally, brands can also use the algorithm to monitor customer sentiment over longer periods of time, making changes accordingly and adjusting marketing campaigns, or products, to suit.

Save time and money with AI targeted advertising

AI can be used to create targeted ads by analysing customer data and finding patterns in order to make the advertising process more efficient and effective.

For example, AI can quickly gather data about potential customers, as well as their interests and preferences which can then be used to create targeted ads that are more likely to be of interest to the customer, and thus more likely to result in a sale.

In addition, AI can also be used to help track the results of those targeted ads and monitor how customers are responding to it in real-time. This means that marketers will be able to quickly identify which ads are most effective and which ones need to be tweaked in order to improve results. This feedback can then be used to further refine future advertising campaigns, making them even more successful.

The efficient nature of this intelligent and instantaneous process allows the potential to not only save time, but also save money on advertising expenses while drastically improving ROI.

A new era of personalised marketing

As AI continues to evolve, it will have an increasingly profound impact on marketing, which can help marketers create even more personalised and relevant experiences for individual customers.

Many are predicting that new forms of personalisation will increase in advertising and marketing efforts in the years ahead due to the advances in Web 3.0 technology.

In the near future customers may not have to read an entire website to find the information that's relevant to them and what they're looking for. With the help of advanced data and insights, brands can create tailored and personal experiences for their customers including website content that can change every time a user visits a page, or even display an entirely different page based on the interests of the user.

Personalisation such as this is already possible, particularly with e-mail technology that allows brands to create targeted e-mail campaigns based on what links someone clicks on. The more links a user clicks, the more personalised content they will receive that is catered to their specific interests.

For example, an online clothing store can learn that a potential customer is only interested in sports attire. With the right AI integration, the next time that potential customer returns, the store might automatically display content and UGC that showcases their sports attire. Without any extra searching, the potential customer can learn how comfortable their sports attire is when working out, and how other customers are enjoying the product; while removing any competing content that mentions other products the customer clearly isn't interested in (yet).

Using AI to predict future customer behaviour

This is perhaps one of the most powerful applications of AI in marketing. Predicting what the customer wants, when they will want it, and why they will want it has long been the goal for marketers new and old.

Thanks to AI, if a business has collected enough data from their customers, they can start to implement complex equations that help identify different patterns or changes in buyer behaviour.

By analysing past customer behaviour, businesses can use predictive analytics to better target their advertising and make better decisions about future marketing campaigns based on the customers' actions.

The potential of this is enormous, as we know from Target and their baby-prediction techniques, and could be one of the most transformational uses of AI data-analysis of our time. AI predictive analysis has the power to automatically alert marketers when an individual has reached a critical point in their journey when they are most likely to consider that brand or business.

There are so many likely scenarios in which AI may be able to predict marketing opportunities ahead of time. This will lead to greater message cut-through, in conjunction with targeted advertising and increased likelihood of repeat business.

Content creation within seconds

A truly transformative way of creating content is already here.

Gone are the days of trawling through stock image libraries, or relaying briefs to photographers and graphic designers or creators. Today, there are already a number of popular AI services such as Dall-E and Midjourney which allow instant image generation that can be used to create custom social media content, product photos, surreal imagery and so much more.

This can enable businesses to create bespoke content and imagery without having to spend money on photo shoots, graphical artists or editing software. The time that this can save marketers in getting a campaign off the ground is huge, and we expect to see more innovations in this space in the not-too-distant future.

Midjourney and Dall-E use a type of Artificial Intelligence referred to as a "generative adversarial network" (GAN) to create images from text descriptions and prompts that are supplied by the user.

Suppose, for example, that you asked it to "draw a picture of a cat riding a skateboard", it would produce an image that looked realistic enough to fool even the most discerning viewer.

For the AI to be able to do this, it first "learns" how to recognize different objects and scenes from a large dataset of images, such as the imageNet database. As soon as the program has been trained, it can then create images based on the textual descriptions and requests it receives.

How the 'Internet of Things' will change the way we live

In a time when AI is increasingly infiltrating our lives and technology continues to evolve exponentially, it's no surprise that the so-called 'Internet of Things' is quickly becoming a major talking point among brands and marketers alike.

The Internet of Things basically refers to technology that would allow everyday objects to be connected to the Internet and to each other, so that they can collect and share data that would be of benefit to the end user.

This includes everything from appliances and cars to wearable devices and even buildings. Imagine what it would mean if your car could communicate with traffic signals to help you avoid congestion, or if your fridge could order more milk when it detects that you're running low.

This is a reality where the opportunities are endless and we are already staring directly into a future that seems remarkably similar to something out of a Steven Spielberg film. This in turn will have a huge impact on marketing, where businesses will be able to collect vast amounts of data about consumers' personal habits and preferences. This will allow them to target advertising in much more subtle yet effective ways.

Some people have rightly raised concerns about the privacy implications of the Internet of Things, but if used correctly, this technology has the potential to improve our lives in countless ways. Especially so if we consider the role that cryptocurrencies and pay-to-play advertising could have in this future.

Making friends in virtual communities

Virtual communities have long since been common-place on the Internet and some of which are still active to this day. As one of the foundational experiences of Web 1.0, this is a trend that is intrinsically related to the natural human desire to belong.

A virtual community called The WELL (Whole Earth 'Lectronic Link) was one of the most popular places to be on the web in the early 1990's. In fact, Wired Magazine even once called it "the world's most influential online community".[1]

Online and virtual communities like The WELL encouraged member interaction, often focusing around a particular interest or just as a place to communicate and share information. Community members interact through various means such as social media, forums, chat rooms, or virtual/gaming worlds. Users from all around the world contribute and create content for their online communities in the form of entertainment, advice, ideas and more.

In recent years, a Reddit group called 'Wall-StreetBets' captured the attention of the financial world. What started as a forum for retail investors to share stock tips and trading ideas has morphed into a full-fledged rebellion against the establishment. From taking on hedge funds to driving up the prices of forgotten stocks, the members of WallStreetBets have shown that they are a force to be reckoned with and they're setting their sights on becoming a powerful force in investing.

In just a few short months, WallStreetBets has gone from being an obscure corner of the Internet to becoming a household name. The group has been credited with causing major disruptions in the markets, and their influence is only growing.

This demonstrates both the potential power that these virtual communities can hold in the real world, and also the passion behind a forum or community that is united by a common interest.

Brands should consider entering these virtual communities, not to sell or market themselves, but to have conversations and be an ear to those in the community because there is much that marketers can learn firsthand about the consumer. That's not to say that brands need to go undercover with an alias and pretend to be someone or something they're not, instead they should be proud to showcase themselves by fostering discussions on topics related to their core brand values and purpose.

This in turn will help build trust in the eyes of the consumer, while positioning the brand in a whole new light and providing their marketing teams with firsthand data to be able to make more informed decisions.

We already know that Web 3.0 aims to be an integrated way of connecting life and the Internet, and establishing a voice early in these virtual communities will ensure that brands will be ready to ride the wave of what's to come.

What to do now?

Looking ahead, brands need to remember why people buy the product or service that they are marketing. At the end of the day, people don't just buy because of the quality of the product anymore, they buy because of the meaning that the product represents.

There's a reason why counterfeit Rolex watches continue to exist after decades of stringent busts and arrests. It's because Rolex as a brand sells status, and even a Rolex copy will give the wearer a distinctive feeling.

It's been demonstrated time and again that people will often buy based on emotion, then justify their decision with logic. We may usually buy because of the status that we will gain, the feelings that we will feel, or the meaning that the product carries.

Brands like Patagonia and Kathmandu don't just sell quality outdoor wear, they sell adventure. The same can be said for makeup newcomer Fenty, who don't just sell quality makeup, they sell inclusivity for all skin tones, marketing themselves as a diverse brand for a diverse customer base.

Unlike the major makeup brands, Fenty creates products for women whose skin tones do not fall into the ranges they typically target or focus on. Because of this Fenty excelled at doing what other beauty brands have been struggling with for years – connecting with people on an emotional and physical level.

It won't be long before user-generated content and AI-generated content are indistinguishable from one another, which may raise suspicions as to whether there's a human or a computer on the other end of marketing messages.

Throughout society, there has been a long-held concern that AI automation would eliminate all of our jobs. Fears of its implications and power over our lives have spawned a giant wave of political, social, and economic questions about our current time and the future that we are heading towards.

Is AI going to enable business owners to be so productive that they can offer a higher standard of living to their employees? Could a powerful enough AI and a lot of computing power allow a single person to create most of the content online?

These questions and more are being asked all around the world. However, it's important to note that AI is not a complete replacement for humans when it comes to content creation. Instead, AI can be used as a powerful tool to augment the creative process and make it easier for people to create high-quality content and allows for more efficient content creation by streamlining the workflow process and reducing the amount of time needed to complete a task.

By utilising machine learning algorithms and artificial intelligence, marketers can explore more options and come up with creative solutions to complex problems.

Ultimately, AI will not replace human creativity. Instead, it provides us with powerful tools that we can use to create even better content. As technology advances and AI becomes more advanced, the possibilities for what it can be used to create will expand exponentially. We are only beginning to explore the potential that AI-generated content has for us today, but we should expect to see much more in the near future.

There are billions of people all around the world who are using the Internet increasingly more in their day-to-day lives, all of which have their own interests, thoughts and beliefs. It should be our collective hope that AI automation only pushes us to do better and help benefit our fellow human beings.

If brands remain 'human' and conscious of their values, while understanding the common interests of the consumer, they can really champion change in Web 3.0 and propel their business long into the future.

REFERENCES

Foreword

1, 2 Internet World Stats – www.internetworldstats.com/stats.htm. (2022). Miniwatts Marketing Group. Retrieved from https://www.internetworldstats.com/emarketing.htm

3 Winnick, M., Mons, J. (2022). “Putting a Finger on Our Phone Obsession. Mobile touches: a study on how humans use technology”. Dscout. Retrieved from https://dscout.com/people-nerds/mobile-touches

Chapter One

1 Mohammad, Y. (October 29, 2022). “How Many Websites use Google Analytics 2022: Google Analytics Statistics”. Renlon.com. Retrieved from https://www.renolon.com/google-analytics-statistics/

Chapter Two

1 U.S. Department of Labor, Bureau of Labor Statistics Summary (99-4 March 1999). “Computer Ownership Up Sharply in the 1990s”. Issues in Labor Statistics. Retrieved from https://www.bls.gov/opub/btn/archive/computer-ownership-up-sharply-in-the-1990s.pdf

2 Pelline, J. (January 3, 1998). “Microsoft Buys Hotmail”. CNET. Retrieved June 11, 2020. Retrieved from https://en.wikipedia.org/wiki/Outlookcom

3 Lafrance, A. (April 21, 2017). “The First-Ever Banner Ad on the Web”. The Atlantic. Retrieved from https://www.theatlantic.com/technology/archive/2017/04/the-first-ever-banner-ad-on-the-web/523728/

Chapter Three

1, 2 Duhigg, C. (February 16, 2012). "How Companies Learn Your Secrets". The New York Times Magazine. Retrieved from https://www.nytimes.com/2012/02/19/magazine/shopping-habits.html?pagewanted=1&_r=1&hp

Chapter Four

1, 2 Gunn, D. (September 9, 2021). "The History of Blogging: From 1997 Until Now". Themeisle. Retrieved from https://themeisle.com/blog/history-of-blogging/

3, 4 Santora, J. (December 19, 2022). "Key Influencer Marketing Statistics to Drive Your Strategy in 2023". Influencer Marketing Hub. Retrieved from https://influencermarketinghub.com/influencer-marketing-statistics/

Chapter Five

1, 2, 3 Kemp, S. (January 26, 2022). "Digital 2022: Time Spent Using Connected Tech Continues to Rise". DataReportal. Retrieved from https://datareportal.com/reports/digital-2022-time-spent-with-connected-tech

4 Bhaskar Chakravorti et al. (February 25, 2021). "How Digital Trust Varies Around the World". Harvard Business Review. Retrieved from https://hbr.org/2021/02/how-digital-trust-varies-around-the-world

Chapter Six

1 Jones, E. (July 7, 2020). "Generation Influence: Gen Z Study Reveals a New Digital Paradigm". Business Wire. Retrieved from https://www.businesswire.com/news/home/20200706005543/en/Generation-Influence-Gen-Z-Study-Reveals-a-New-Digital-Paradigm

2 Selig, A. (December 9, 2022). "Generation Influence: Reaching Gen Z in the New Digital Paradigm". WP Engine. Retrieved from https://wpengine.com/resources/gen-z-2020-full-report/

Chapter Seven

1 VloggerGear.com. (December 19, 2022). "How Much Does Mr. Beast Make? [2023 Net Worth + Earnings]". Vloggergear. Retrieved from https://vloggergear.com/how-much-does-mr-beast-make/

2 Capitalism.com. (November 14, 2022). "What is MrBeast's Net Worth? His Billionaire YouTube Career and Philanthropy". Capitalism.com. Retrieved from https://www.capitalism.com/what-is-mrbeasts-net-worth/

3 CoinMarketCap BTC Price Live Data. Figures are current as at 1 January 2023. Retrieved from https://coinmarketcap.com/currencies/bitcoin/

Chapter Eight

1 Gitte Lindgaard, Gary Fernandes, Cathy Dudek & J. Brown (2006). "Attention web designers: You have 50 milliseconds to make a good first impression!". Behaviour & In formation Technology, 25:2, 115-126, DOI: 10.1080/01449290500330448. Taylor & Frances Online. Retrieved from https://www.tandfonline.com/doi/abs/10.1080/01449290500330448

Chapter Nine

1, 2 Dimaculangan, J. Kraus, E. (July 28, 2022). "31 Branding Statis tics Every Small Business Should Know in 2022". Fit Small Business. Retrieved from https://fitsmallbusiness.com/brand ing-statistics/

Chapter Ten

1 Ha, A. (April 25, 2020). "Fortnite hosted a psychedelic Travis Scott concert and 12.3M people watched". TechCrunch. Retrieved from https://techcrunch.com/2020/04/24/fortnite-hosted-a-psychedelic-travis-scott-concert-and-12-3m-people-watched/

2 Goncharenko, V. (May 30, 2022). "Gucci creates a Town in Roblox". Metaverse Post. Retrieved from https://mpost.io/gucci-creates-a-town-in-roblox/

3 TFL Editorial Team. (May 25, 2021). "A Digital-Only Gucci Bag Sold for $4,115 on Roblox, as Brands Continue to Look to Gaming to Reach Gen-Z". The Fashion Law. Retrieved from https://www.thefashionlaw.com/a-digital-only-gucci-bag-sold-for-4115-on-roblox-as-brands-continue-to-look-to-gaming-as-reach-gen-z/

4 Rinker, H. (January 13, 2002). "Coca-Cola bottle-cap promo tions date back to the 1950s and "60s". The Morning Call. Retrieved from https://www.mcall.com/news/mc-xpm-2002-01-13-3740182-story.html

5, 6 MMA Global Case Study Editorial Team. (2014). "McDonald's Australia: McDonald's Monopoly App". Mobile Marketing Association. Retrieved from https://www.mmaglobal.com/case-study-hub/case_studies/view/46445

7 Tieryas, P. (August 18, 2017). "Nintendo's Tour of the Louvre: Gaming, Art, and Virtual Reality". Tor.com. Retrieved from https://www.tor.com/2017/08/18/nintendos-tour-of-the-louvre-gaming-art-and-virtual-reality/

8 Alsop, T. (March 30, 2022). "Augmented reality (AR) market size worldwide in 2017, 2018 and 2025". Statista. Retrieved from https://www.statista.com/statistics/897587/world-augmented-reality-market-value/

Chapter Eleven

1 Hafner, K. (May 1, 1997). "The Epic Saga of The Well: The World's Most Influential Online Community (And It's Not AOL)". Wired. Retrieved March 18, 2022. https://www.wired.com/1997/05/ff-well/